Couples

A hot little book about us.

havoc

PUBLISHING

©1997 Havoc Publishing

ISBN 1-57977-104-1

Published and created by Havoc Publishing

San Diego, California

First Printing, May 1997

Designed by Juddesign

Some images © 1997 PhotoDisc, Inc.

Printed in China

Please write to us for more information on our

Havoc Publishing Record Books and Products.

HAVOC PUBLISHING

7868 Silverton Avenue, Suite A

San Diego, California 92126

Couples

A hot little book about us

A record book for

_____ & _____

Contents

All About Us

In the Beginning & Our First Date

Photographs

Our First Kiss

Our Most Exciting & Miserable Dates

I Knew I Loved You When & Saying the "L" Word

Meeting the Parents

Trips

Photographs

Tokens of Affection

Celebrations

The First Item We Purchased Together

Photographs

Our Differences & Similarities

Best Personality Traits & Physical Attributes

Contents

Memorabilia

Affectionate Pet Names

Love Notes

Things We Should Just Do Alone

Favorite Rainy Day Activities

The Best of Times...

Feast on This

Favorite Recipe & Menu

Song and Dance

Nights At Home

Out on the Town

Programs & Ticket Stubs

What I've Always Wanted to Tell You

Photographs

Our Future

All About Us

Her career

_____

_____

Her hobbies and interests

_____

_____

_____

How she relaxes

_____

_____

His career

_____

_____

His hobbies and interests

_____

_____

_____

How he relaxes

_____

_____

In The Beginning

How we met
_____

_____

_____

Where we met
_____

_____

What attracted us to each other
_____

_____

First impressions
_____

_____

_____

How long before we went out
_____

_____

Our First Date

When _____

Where we went _____

Who asked whom _____

Best part of the date _____

_____

_____

We were most nervous about _____

_____

Who called whom first _____

Photograph

Photograph

Our First Kiss

When _____

Where _____

Who kissed whom _____

We'll always remember _____

_____

_____

_____

_____

Photo

Our Most Exciting Date

When

Where we went

What made it so exciting

Our Most Miserable Date

When _____

Where we went _____

Why it was so miserable _____

_____

_____

_____

_____

_____

_____

I Knew I Loved You When...

Saying The "L" Word

Who said it first _____

When _____

Where _____

_____

His reaction _____

_____

_____

Her reaction _____

_____

_____

Dad picture here

Mom picture here

Meeting The Parents

His

When _____

Where _____

_____

What we did _____

_____

_____

How it went _____

_____

_____

_____

Hers

When
_____

Where
_____
_____

What we did
_____
_____
_____

How it went
_____
_____
_____
_____

Mom picture here

Dad picture here

Our First Trip

When _____

Where _____

What happened along the way _____

_____

_____

Our Favorite Trip

When _____

Where _____

What we did _____

_____

_____

Our Most Romantic Getaway

When _____

Where _____

Why it was so romantic _____

_____

_____

_____

_____

_____

_____

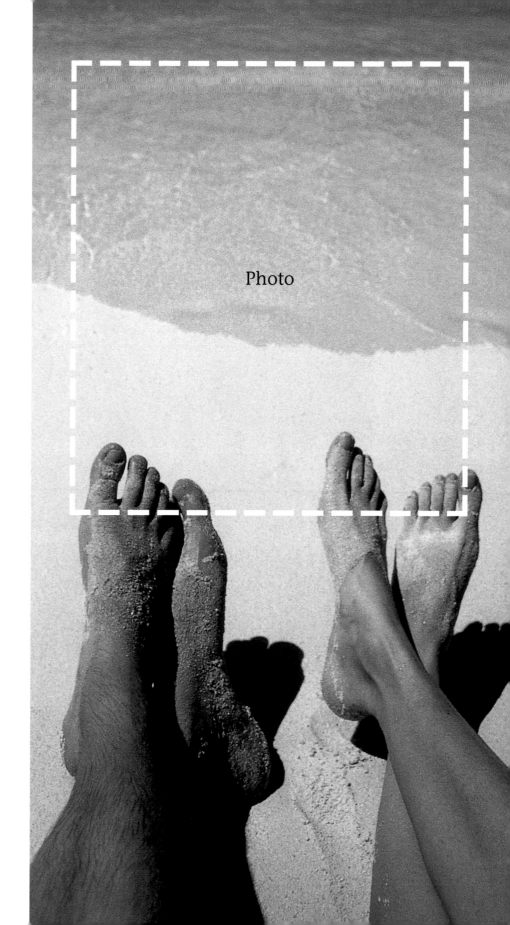

Photo

Photograph

Photograph

Tokens of Affection

The first gift he gave her
_____

_____

His favorite gift
_____

Why
_____

_____

_____

The most romantic gift
_____

_____

The first gift she gave him
_____

_____

Her favorite gift
_____

Why
_____

_____

_____

The most romantic gift
_____

_____

celebrations

His birthday

_____

_____

Her birthday

_____

_____

Anniversaries

_____

_____

_____

Holidays

_____

_____

Other special events

_____

_____

How we spend them

_____

_____

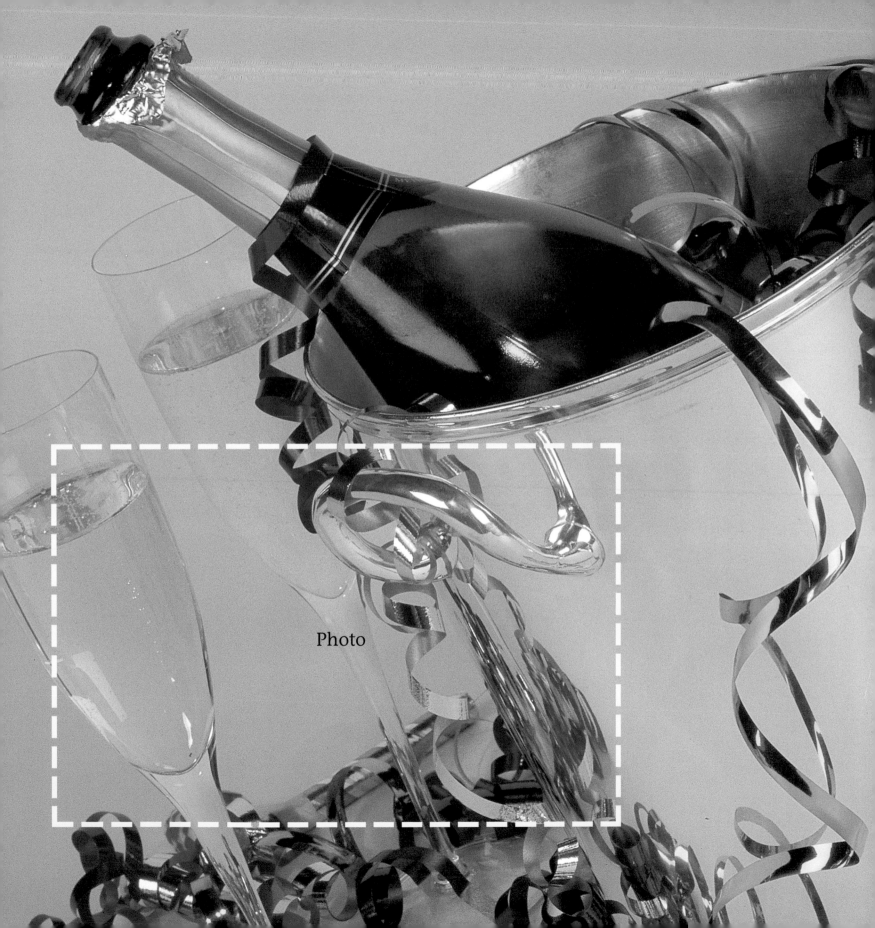

Photo

The First Item
We Purchased Together

Item _____

When _____

Where _____

How much _____

Reason _____

_____

_____

_____

Photograph

Photograph

Our Differences

Our Similarities

_____

_____

_____

_____

_____

_____

_____

What he loves most about her

_____

_____

_____

_____

Best Personality Traits

What she loves most about him

_____

_____

_____

_____

_____

His _____

_____

_____

_____

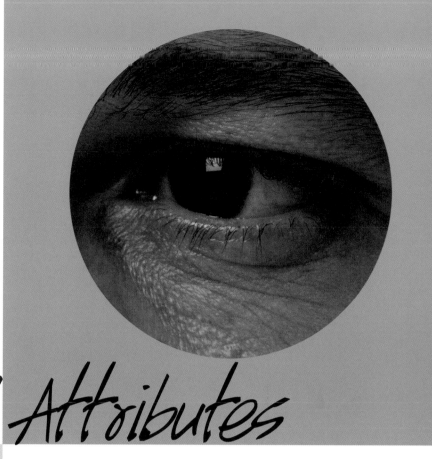

Best Physical Attributes

Hers _____

_____

_____

_____

_____

_____

Memorabilia

Memorabilia

Affectionate Pet Names

honey

She sometimes calls him _____

_____

_____

_____

He sometimes calls her _____

_____

_____

_____

_____

sweetie

sugar

darlin' love

doll

muffin punkin'

pookey babe

Things We Should Just Do Alone

His activities
_____
_____
_____
_____
_____

Her activities
_____
_____
_____
_____

Favorite Ways To Spend Time Together

_____

_____

_____

_____

_____

_____

_____

_____

_____

_____

Favorite Rainy Day Activities

Outdoors

_____

_____

_____

_____

_____

Indoors

_____

_____

_____

_____

The Best of Times...

The Worst of Times

Photo

Feast On This

Favorite meal

_____

First meal he cooked for her

First meal she cooked for him

Favorite dessert

Foods he introduced to her

_____

_____

Foods she introduced to him

_____

_____

Favorite Recipe

Favorite Menu

Our song _____

Why _____

_____

Our first dance _____

When _____

Where _____

Song _____

His favorite group _____

_____

Music she introduced to him _____

_____

Her favorite group _____

_____

Music he introduced to her _____

_____

Nights At Home

Our favorite activities _____

Our favorite meals _____

Our Favorite Rentals

Our favorite treats _____

VHS
VHS
VHS
VHS
VHS

Out On The Town

Our favorite activities _____

_____

Our favorite restaurants _____

Our favorite dance clubs _____

Our favorite theatres _____

Our favorite plays/musicals _____

_____

New places he introduced to her _____

_____

New places she introduced to him _____

_____

426003

ADMIT ONE

Ticket Stubs

ADMIT ONE

426002

what i've

Always Wanted
To Tell You

Photograph

Photograph